OUR MISSION AND PURPOSE:

OUR INTENT AND PURPOSE FOR BEING HERE IS TO PRESENT THE GOSPEL OF THE LORD JESUS CHRIST THROUGH THIS MEDIUM AROUND THE WORLD. OUR GOAL IS TO REACH AS MANY PEOPLE AND NATIONS AS POSSIBLE WITH THIS "GOOD NEWS."

AS CHRISTIANS, WE ARE NEVER ASHAMED TO REACH INTO CULTURES, POLITICAL PERSUASIONS AND NATIONS IN THE SHARING OF THIS GOSPEL MESSAGE. WE ABSOLUTELY BELIEVE THAT WE ARE PLACED HERE ON THE EARTH IN THIS POSITION TO HAVE AN EFFECT UPON TODAY'S SOCIETY. AND WE WILL NEVER BE ASHAMED OF THIS GREAT MESSAGE AND PURPOSE.

THE EDITOR AND PUBLISHER

Charles Lingerfelt

CTM & North Texas Freedom Rally

Proverbs 2:6
For the LORD gives wisdom; from his mouth come knowledge and understanding

ISSN 2639-7714 (PRINT)
ISSN: 2639-7730 (ONLINE)

Charles Lingerfelt
Editor In Chief

Publisher
Christian Times Magazine &
North Texas Freedom Rally

Graphic & Interior Design
Saba Jenn & Anil Anwar

I BLEED RED, WHITE, & BLUE

CHRISTIAN TIMES MAGAZINE
ISSUE 62 | AUG 2022

Published & Printed in the United States of America

Christian Times Magazine is underwritten by NORTH TEXAS FREEDOM RALLY with Headquarters in Dallas, Texas USA

Copyright © 2022 by Christian Times Magazine
Note: Our content is available for free

christiantimesmag@gmail.com

EDITOR'S NOTE

'The Russian Bear' has made its move down out of the North and is beginning to growl. 'The Chinese Dragon' may spew its fire even quicker than we think.

But soon and very soon we will hear the roar of the Lion of the tribe of Judah. It's not over yet, but we can see the closeness of the Lord. Be still, stay calm, stand firm! As He begins His "roaring," EVERYTHING is being shaken and will fall into place:

John invokes us to understand the way God/Yahweh spoke when He gave the Torah at Mount Sinai. Psalm 68:8 recalls this event as "one where the ground shook at His words."

The following statement, beginning with "Yet once more…" is a quotation from Haggai 2:6, where God offers a long-term prophecy of His eventual remaking of all of creation. (Revelation 21:1)

"The LORD Himself will fight for you. Just stay calm." (Exodus 14:14)

Be still, stay calm, stand firm. As He is roaring, EVERYTHING is being shaken. (Hebrews 12:27) our kingdom, a spiritual kingdom CANNOT be shaken!

"The hand of the LORD was upon me, and carried me out in the spirit of the LORD, and set me down in the midst of the valley which was full of bones, And caused me to pass by them round about: and, behold, there were very many in the open valley; and, lo, they were very dry. (Ezekiel 37:1-14)

And God told Ezekiel to 'prophesy unto these bones.' Ezekiel obeyed God and prophesied over those dry bones. And in our day and time, in my own beautiful day of youthfulness, we saw the nation of Israel come together, reunite and "be born in a day" to become a leading nation, A powerful nation in the Middle East. This is prophecy fulfilled!

To God be all the glory…

Standby my friend, be patient, be alert and be calm...

God is about to 'Show Himself!'

Charles Lingerfelt
Editor-in-Chief
CTM - Christian Times Magazine

'THE MOST CHRISTIAN CONSERVATIVE MAGAZINE IN AMERICA!'

CHRISTIAN TIMES MAGZINE
CONTENTS

CHRISTIAN TIMES MAGAZINE ISSUE 62

06 **EXCLUSIVE!**
THE PROPHECIES OF JOEL
BY CHARLES LINGERFELT

11 THEY TAKE OUR LIBERTY AND GIVE US DEATH
BY KATHERINE DAIGLE

17 KNOWING & FINDING GOD
BY J. K. HARRILL

23 RIGHTING THE SHIP?!
BY CHRIS GRAHN HOWARD

29 A CHANGE OF HEART BY GOD THE GREAT CARDIOLOGIST
BY DR. GEORGETTE NICHOLS

36 MENTORS , LEADERS, TEACHERS AND GUIDES:
THE VALUE OF MENTORING IN A CHRISTIAN PERSPECTIVE
BY ZERNALYN PALMARES

40 THIS AND THAT
BY MICKEY NICHOLS

43 INTERVIEW WITH PAUL MANGO
TRUMP'S WHITE HOUSE FORMER DEPUTY CHIEF OF STAFF FOR POLICY

AUG | ISSUE **62**

CHRISTIANTIMESMAG@GMAIL.COM

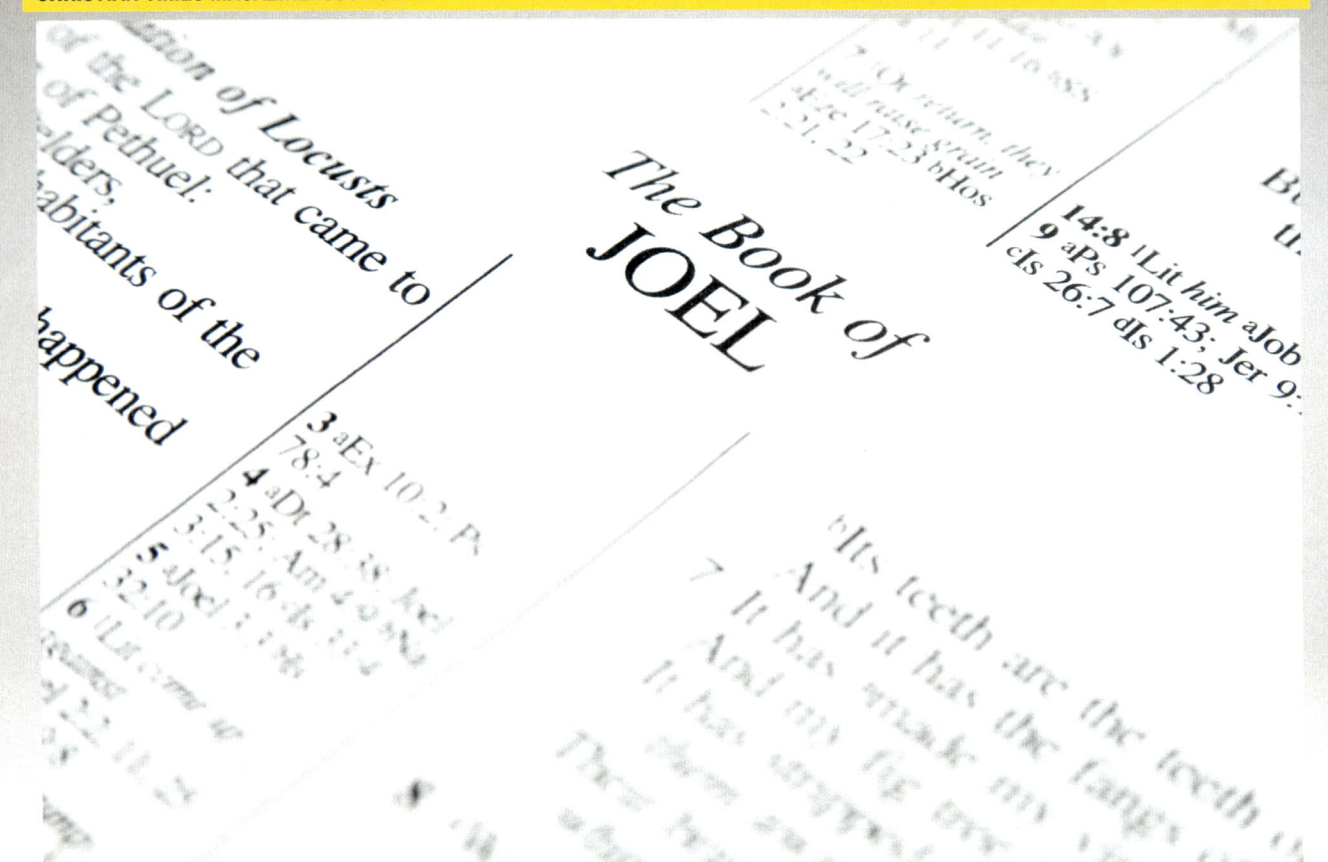

The Prophecies of Joel

By Charles Lingerfelt

The book of Joel is a brief prophetic book of the Old Testament that predicted the outpouring of the Holy Spirit upon all people in the end-time - it was a prophecy that was fulfilled several centuries later on the day of Pentecost (Joel 2:28-32; Acts 2:14-21). The title of the book comes from its author, Joel, whose name means, 'Jehovah is God.'

That 'outpouring' is yet being fulfilled today in our time; and "upon our sons and daughters" the Holy Spirit is still being poured forth.

In the first section of the book, Joel calls attention to a devastating swarm of locusts that had recently swept through the land (1:4). These destructive locusts stripped the foliage from all trees, shrubs, and crops (1:7). The people and livestock of Judah were facing the threat of starvation because of the famine that followed this invasion (1:15-18). As bad as this natural catastrophe had been, the prophet declares it will be as nothing in comparison to the coming day of the Lord. This is the coming Day of JUDGMENT, when God will vent his wrath upon his disobedient and sinful people. Joel also informs the people that this terrible day can be avoided. The way of escape is to turn to God "with all your heart, with fasting and with mourning" (2:12).

After Joel delivers his pleas for repentance, God Himself speaks to his wayward people. In spite of the famine, He declares that there will be plenty to eat in the days of blessing to come (2:18,19). This day of renewal will be marked by the outpouring of His spirit upon all people (2:28,29). All the nations of the world will take notice as God gathers His 'chosen people' together in the holy city of Jerusalem to serve as their ruler: "Judah shall abide forever, and Jerusalem from generation to generation" (3:20).

The Prophet Joel identifies himself in the introduction as "the son of Pethuel" (1:1). This is about all we know about this spokesman for the Lord. From evidence in the book itself, we can assume that the prophet knew a great deal about Jerusalem, Judah's capital city, and the rituals associated with temple worship (2:15). But he probably was not a priest, since he called upon the priests to go into mourning because of the sins of the nation (1:13). Indeed, Joel's many references to agriculture (1:7, 10-12) may quite probably indicate that he was a farmer or a herdsman, although that is not certain.

It is difficult to determine the exact date of the writing of this book. Unlike most of the other Old Testament prophets, Joel mentions no kings of Judah or Israel and no historical events that might give us some indication about when he wrote his prophetical book. The one strong clue is the similarity of Joel's concept of 'the Day of the Lord' to the language of the prophet Zephaniah (Joel 2:2; Zephaniah 1:14-16). Zephaniah prophesied shortly before the fall of Jerusalem and the nation of Judah in 587 B.C. This also seems to be the most likely time for the writing of the book of Joel. If Joel did in fact write his book about 600 B.C., he would have lived in the frantic final years of the nation of Judah. After the Babylonian army destroyed Jerusalem and 587/586 B.C. The leading citizens of Judah where are carried into captivity over into Babylon. This invasion of the Babylonians must have given special significance to the terrible "day of the Lord" about which Joel warned his countrymen.

The book of Joel is a remarkable contribution to Christianity today because it shows that a message from God can often come packaged in the form of a natural disaster. The truth of the book is rooted in the disastrous invasion of locusts, which Joel describes in a powerfully vivid language. This prophet teaches us that the Lord God Almighty may use a natural disaster to stir within the hearts of His people a renewed awareness of His divine will. Any traumatic event of nature - flood, fire, storm, or earthquake - should motivate the sensitive ear to listen again to the words of the Lord.

Readers of Joel's prophetic book are always impressed with his ability to prophetically predict, through the unction of the Holy Spirit of course, the future outpouring of the Holy Spirit (Joel 2:28-32). The Apostle Peter used this passage to explain the exciting events of PENTECOST to his hearers on the Day of Pentecost (Acts 2:16-21). Just as Joel predicted, the Holy Spirit why is poured out on all these early followers of Jesus who were gathered in Jerusalem seeking God's will and praying for His divine guidance.

But there is still a future dimension in Joe's prophecies. The gifts of the Spirit that began to flow through the people of God on Pentecost were not exhausted on that day. They are still available to all who believe in the Lord Jesus Christ and who anxiously await His glorious return in the final establishment of His kingdom.

'Even so, Come Lord Jesus!'

CHRISTIAN TIMES MAGAZINE ENDORSES

SHELLY AKERLY
FOR DALLAS COUNTY TREASURER

www.akerlyfordallas.com

THEY TAKE OUR LIBERTY AND GIVE US DEATH

By Katherine Daigle

Gun rights in this country are under attack, once again. Criminals are allowed to have their freedom, but men women and children still are in FEAR while carnage insurgents create a purge on society.

The Second Amendment was ratified on December 15, 1791, and since that day solidified one of Americans` most fundamental rights – the right to keep and bear arms. So, what does the Amendment mean in simple terms? "The Second Amendment protects an individual right to possess a firearm unconnected with service in a militia, and to use that arm for traditionally lawful purposes, such as self-defense within the home."

The very essence of the Second Amendment is a guarantee that every American citizen has a right to arm themselves, and the Government has no way to infringe on that right. In other words, it guarantees us freedom and independence, the matters that underpin us as a state and a Nation. Fundamentally it is our birth right pledged under the Constitution and has always been a target of the left-leaning bureaucrats. "The right to dissent is marked intricately in the Second Amendment." ("Second Amendment: Representing Freedom and Liberty for All") It provides Americans with a sense of liberty to voice their distrust of tyranny. It gives citizens hope in keeping autocratic decisions at bay. These facts do not take away the key tenet of responsibility that this right demands from its beneficiaries either. It is important to note that a ban on arms will not spell the end of violence – other methods are key in dismantling the system of destruction that people often resort to in cases where there have been outbreaks of violence to control the masses under these politicians who need power. Instances of mass shootings can be prevented but will never be eliminated. The cause of such mayhem must be countered and brought down. But that does not translate to methods antagonistic to the Second Amendment.

Our Founding Fathers devised this freedom to safeguard our right to choose, protect and protest when things turn murkier than they ever should. It was never meant to wreak havoc. Therefore, the focus should be on reading the Second Amendment for what it is rather than distorting it to fit a politician's political narrative.

The primary target for reversing pugnacious tendencies in a society should rest on defining the moral and ethical standards of humanity. With people inclining further towards what is morally right and finding the wrongs, it would be possible to put a curb on the destructive urge. This conditioning should begin with early education. Concepts that rely on moral and ethical values should be inculcated in growing children, not for the sake of it but for it to be held onto for the rest of their lives. However, this must not be confused with the arbitrary outlining of what is 'right' and what is 'wrong.' Relative validity matters here as well. Teaching children what is morally acceptable while making sure this is not an arbitrary affirmation of closed thinking is necessary to wage a war against the outbreak of violence. These are solutions that run deep and require an overwhelming effort to be propelled into fruition. Therefore, the immediate demand that people often fall back on is the removal of the Second Amendment from the Constitution. But that can never be the long-term solution. It takes away the core central ideas of liberty and freedom. "If you turn back on one right, the others too will follow suit." Liberals only seem interested in a much-preferred favorite and easy target blame the NRA and "gun control rights. Liberals have turned the gun debate into a "moral push" even though we should be able to find bipartisan and reasonable solutions. Nevertheless, just like many other rights and liberties, this one is being jeopardized particularly harshly. After facing a powerful pushback trying to restrict our rights for assembly, movement, and even expression, turn the education system inside out, and polarize the society on every Constitutional 2nd Amendment, the socialists, Democrats, and RINOS of the republican party lobby in American Government and they seem to have taken a different approach. It looks like they have decided to take our main way to protect our liberties first and then move to restricting freedoms and imposing their narratives one by one. Our rights and our freedoms as Americans should never be up for debate. It is our responsibility as Americans to ensure that we do not give up those rights. Because if history teaches us anything it is this if we ever give up our rights and our freedoms, we will never get them back. No matter what we do, no matter how many laws we pass, we will never fully stop evil people from doing evil things. We don't live in a utopian society.

The reactionary attacks on our Constitution cannot be allowed to go unanswered. Democrats believe that angering Americans results in stark cultural divides between civilians and police, and at worst can provoke more tragedies, and chaos within our country, remember divide and conquer. When the political left begins to cry out that the right is responsible for these weapons, votes will flow to the people who decry the injustices. Of course, this political strategy is not only irresponsible and immoral but also flatly dangerous, particularly since the lockdowns and masks are being reintroduced when naturally, horrible things like that happen, they are spun as evidence of the clear need for "gun control" measures that would strip Americans of their rights.

What is most galling is the rhetoric and the sheer hypocrisy of it? Most of the homicides recently occur at the hands of undocumented immigrants and young gang members flowing into our country, and as such do not fit the necessary political narrative of the Left. Unless, of course, it is time for another round of calls for gun control; then and only then are these killings put on parade, then, those lives seem to matter. The calls for gun control themselves, like most leftist ideas, seem superficially reasonable. We had a horrific shooting, so let's make guns harder to get. That makes sense, right? Frankly, no, it does not – and here is why.

When you talk about "making guns harder to get", you're leaving off the most important part at the end: "for law-abiding Americans." Perpetrators of mass shootings do not care about getting their guns through proper channels. They're happy to get them illegally, just like they apparently are happy to commit murder illegally. All that most "gun control" measures can do is make it so that people who respect the law will be unarmed when these volatile and dangerous monsters show up, guns blazing.

So, what CAN we do? Well, let's start by not turning a blind eye:

"When the administration and President Joe Biden campaigned on the promise to enact pro-criminal policies like no-cash bail, George Soros, a gun-hating, soft-on-crime extremist, saw a major opportunity. On the coattails of the Biden campaign, Soros went to work successfully funding the election of dozens of radical district attorneys across the country. There are now 75 Soros-backed DAs overseeing half of America's 50 most populous cities. They are an astounding one-in-five Americans, and their jurisdictions account for more than 40% of our nation's murders. In a short time, they've transformed our major cities into war zones -Soros-backed, Los Angeles DA George Gascon took office in 2020, and he immediately made radical, pro-criminal changes to prosecution rules, getting rid of sentence enhancements for violent gangs and criminals who commit crimes with guns. The murder rate in LA is up more than 50% since 2019, the year before Gascon took office. Violent robberies are up 60%. Additionally, the citizens of San Francisco voted overwhelmingly to recall Soros-backed DA Chesa Boudin. In a little over two years in office, Boudin's policies have all but destroyed life in the Golden City. Today both Gascon and Boudin have been on a recall list – Boudin was recalled" https://www.americas1stfreedom.org/search?tg=George%20Soros

Defending Our Freedoms, is not "a declaration of war against the entire civilized world" it is not about race, we are all just Americans, fighting for the right to be free under Our Constitution.

The rhetoric of defunding the police found itself under tremendous pressure. People who were as motivated as ever to protect their families and homes have suddenly become a target for aggressive political propaganda that is trying to put the blood of the innocent on the only hands capable of preventing violence in the future. As we have already seen it happening with the reemergence of mandates in advance of our 2022 election and the long-awaited return of SCOTUS (Supreme Court of the United States).

The tragedies in this country during the worldwide economic downturn instigated by globalists have reignited fervent gun control debates across the nation, particularly in relation to the availability of semi-automatic assault weapons, which have been involved in most shootings in the U.S. in recent years. We must wonder why politicians choose to blame guns when things go awry, do they blame electric vehicles when a person is inebriated and kills several bystanders with that vehicle, no. At the same time, The Second Amendment and its guarantees seem to be most relevant and important today. While the rate of unemployment, homelessness, and therefore crime grows tremendously under the current Administration and the "police defunding" calls and practices leave people defenseless against it, your individual right to keep and bear arms might be the only thing that prevents your family from joining the gruesome statistics of violence and crime victims.

While the people stay speechless in the face of irrational hysteria, the administration proposes an "ingenious" idea of making the guns particularly expensive and hard to get. What may seem like a possible solution, at first sight, is, in fact, an attempt to make self-defense and Americans` fundamental right available only to a very narrow circle of the rich and powerful. As a result, it will only turn most American citizens into a faceless mass that can be molded or disposed of at the whim of those who can afford to stay free and protected. And while the Supreme Court has recently backed the right to carry guns in public once again and quashed a New York state that required people to show a particular need to get a license to carry a concealed gun in public, New York appointed Governor Kathy Hochuli and the administration himself openly called the decision "shocking" and "disappointing."

What would you call it if not an admission that the current Administration is trying to deprive us of our birthright guaranteed by the Constitution and the Founding Fathers themselves?

FREEDOM TO DECIDE | FAMILIES FIRST | ACHIEVING DALLAS COUNTY'S FULL POTENTIAL.

ELECT LAUREN DAVIS
FOR DALLAS COUNTY JUDGE

JOIN THE MOVEMENT

HELP ME PUT GOVERNMENT BACK IN ITS PLACE !

Paid for by Lauren Davis Campaign

KNOWING & FINDING GOD

By J. K. Harrill

I remember as a young man attending Vacation Bible School, Indiana Avenue Baptist Church…. MS Ausmus a wonderful woman filled with love for God and his children had talked with me the day before about Jesus and Salvation and Heaven and Forgiveness. I remember standing in almost the same spot that particular day as I had the day before, both days standing with the rest of those attending Bible School that summer. Then as was done every day, just before we were to leave the churches auditorium the Pastor spoke, gave an invitation to come forward, be prayed with and just maybe receive the Lord Jesus Christ as your Savior….. Be Saved.

I stood there that day feeling exactly what I came to know as "Being Under Conviction." Which after some hesitation, eventually led me to walk down the isle of the church, fall down on my knees, Pastor Wells explaining the plan of salvation, praying with me, allowing the Holy Spirit to continue leading me to the place where I began Knowing and Finding God.

I remember the sense of a weight being lifted, a burden which wasn't anything I had really ever felt or had I ever known before, yet once gone everything changed. I immediately began wanting everyone to know who it was that took it away…. I Wanted to Share My Knowing and Finding God. Even though I had grown up in a two-parent home, where I knew my Mothers Parents, My Fathers Mother, Dads Father had died in a tragic automobile accident in 1956. I knew my aunts and Uncles on both sides, knew all my Family went to church, some more than others yet all went. The one thing I had never considered until now…... Did They Know God? Did They Know Where to Find God? If not…. This Newly Saved Soul wanted to tell them exactly what he knew, and how important it was. Excitement that would find some disappointment when learning most already knew…. mostly they were excited, in a few cases I heard their voice breaking, knowing they were brought to tears in hearing of my KNOWING & FINDING GOD.

Over the past fifty-eight years since that day, the day in that altar of Indian Avenue Baptist Church, down on my knees, crying and calling out, asking God to save my soul, I have not always been the best of witnesses or representation of what God personally gave me that day by accepting his Son, Jesus Christ as Lord and Savior. My having been born into this World God created, a part of God's Creation, yet requiring be reborn thus becoming a Child Of The Living God. I have definitely fallen short of those expectations that were planted that day in a child's heart, down on his knees, then standing up finding himself wanting to Save the World.

My Mother's Family names are Richesin, and Lovingood both names of reverence always having been known to Pray. I grew up witnessing as my Family Prayed With, Prayed For and Prayed Directly To God especially at meal time. I can still hear my Grandfather Richesin calling out before a meal was eaten….. "Thelma, Return Thanks!" Thelma was Papaws Wife, my mothers, Mother, and my Mamaw. Mamaw prayers always gave cause to know where the needs of her Family were found, both Physical Family and Church Family. The one guarantee when everyone raised their bowed heads back up after Mamaw said "In The Precious Name Of Your Son Jesus, AMEN AND AMEN…. You Knew Mamaw Knew God.

There were four children born to the marriage of Thelma Lovingood and Jackson Richesin, three daughters and one son. The first born a daughter, next would be a son, then the birth of my mother next, then another daughter. As these were born oldest to youngest, they would pass away youngest to oldest. My Aunt being the last in 2018, two weeks shy of her ninety eighth birthday.

The final two and a half years of my aunt's life, I lived with her, caring for her 20 hours a day, seven days a week. A lady came each day to care for my aunt from 9:00 in the morning until 1:00 in the afternoon, seven days a week. While staying with and caring for this aunt, this last one of the two sisters to my mother, this last member of an entire generation, Her Generation and the last of my lifeline left to That Generation Gone. It is then I really came to "Knowing and Finding God" in a place void of time, with an awareness unexplainable to the human mind, yet Perfectly Communicated By The Heart.

The last year of my aunt's life did not find her present in the place and time we shared. She never made it to 1959 her last year and the reason I know this is because her and my uncle returned home from a Life of Service to our nation in the United States Navy in 1959. A life of service that began in 1936, post WWI and was winding down to retirement in 1959 when they built their new home. The home I moved into to care for my aunt so she would be able to live out her life at home. The home her and my uncle who passed away in 2000 shared, yet now my aunt awoke every day of the last year of life, not recognizing her being home. So, you see I know she never made it up to 1959 that last year. She would awake some mornings and share after I fixed her breakfast, she had to catch the trolley up town to work. I then knew she was in San Francisco that morning and the year was about 1945. Other days she would awake giving a report of the weather, "Well It's Raining Again Today, Rains Most Every Day, Please Get My Rain Bonnet and Umbrella for Me Before We Go Out" from the weather I knew she was in Seattle and the year was about 1947.

She most always gave little hints, sometimes the hint may take us to New Orleans, other times Norfolk or Washington DC where her husband, my uncle had been a Officer at the Pentagon before Retirement, hints of those places just to mention a few that allowed me find and usually join her there. From time to time, she would ask when her Mamaw was coming to get her so she could go home. Those locations and times were emotionally charged connections because I knew she was a mere ten years old when her grandmother passed away, so this Physically Ninety-Eight-Year-Old Lady was now a Seven or Eight or Nine year old young girl who could not grasp why her Grandmother had left her with a stranger. During times such as this i was amazed by the information which had been filed away in my mind, available upon demand providing a roadmap to who and where my aunt was at the different exits in life's journey.

The affect of Alzheimer's and Dementia during that last year of my aunt's life made it impossible for her to know who I really was, she would think me to be her Physician, or a Nurse, a Repairman, a Meter Reader, a Postal Worker…. each having a bit of reality to the work required in caring for her yet she never knew her nephew. Her sisters only son whose wife afforded him the ability to live with and care for her in her home rather than the Nursing Home option.

One of the hardest parts of my aunts Alzheimer's and Dementia, (What I came to call…. Dee and Al, which when people would ask about how my aunt was, I would reply that she has this couple, a woman and man who are her Best Friends, Dee and Al are their names. One thing for sure Dee and Al are always going somewhere, or doing something. Dee and Al come by unannounced, pick up my aunt, take her with them without telling me where they are going or when they are coming back. I always find my aunt, yet Dee and Al definitely don't make it easy! Most everyone who I share this with realized the facts being we have to find humor during the worst of times because that is when we surely need it most.) my aunt would cycle thru times of staying awake for days, two, three, four days without measurable sleep.

It was during one of those times that brought me to this place in writing for you the reality found by me about ten O'clock one night as my aunt was transitioning from her fourth into her fifth day of being awake. I heard my aunt talking to someone, so I went to stand in the doorway, as I often did watching and listening for a while. This particular night shortly after positioning myself in the doorway just out of sight, my aunt clasps her hands together in front of her face as she lay there. She then began to pray, praying for hours, not one hour, not two hours, hours she prayed.

This woman who never had children of her own began praying for The Children…. asking God to comfort and care for the children, quoting scriptures such as "Blessed Be The Children…." and on and on. Then she began praying for the Parents of the children, praying…. "God please help the parents to not bring their children to anger." I was listening to her quoting the Bible…. It Was All Right There to Look Up in The Book and my aunt is Quoting Scriptures While Praying for hours. Next, she prayed for the Laypeople of the Church, then The Pastor, The Body of The Church, The Community Around the Church, The Cities, Counties, States, Nation and World. At the beginning of my Aunts Praying, I had called my wife on the cell phone so she could hear my aunts' prayers that night. Never knowing the extent of her conversation with God or the reality of Knowing and Finding God discovered while listening.

My Aunt did not know me, nor did she know where we were, yet She Knew God, Who God Was, What God Said and Where To Find God! You see the day as a young man attending Bible School, I walked down the isle of Indiana Avenue Baptist Church, dropped down on my knees, accepting the Lord Jesus Christ as my Savior…. God Entered My Heart! Not My Mind…. My Heart!

My Aunt knew exactly where to Find God…. Because God was right there where God had been since the moment when she accepted the Lord Jesus Christ as Her Savior! She didn't have to rely on the brain's thinking, Just Her Heart's KNOWING & FINDING GOD.

CHRISTIAN TIMES MAGAZINE
ENDORSES SID MILLER

SID MILLER
TEXAS AGRICULTURE COMMISSIONER

WEBSITE: WWW.MILLERFORTEXAS.COM
FACEBOOK PAGE: WWW.FACEBOOK.COM/MILLERFORTEXAS
TWITTER: @MILLERFORTEXAS

RIGHTING THE SHIP?!

By Chris Grahn Howard

I am often asked, "How can we turn this Country around?" Great question. More often than not, it is precisely what you think…just not how you might think. This list may appear random, but I will try and tie it all together at the end. I say this because it is as simple and as complicated as one might imagine. How do we get back to some common values? How do we return to a place where both sides (there are far more than two) can honestly sit down and work together? Where have all the statesmen gone? These questions only beg for more questions. I could spend time blaming one side for this

Let's get one thing clear. No one side, ideology, or party owns the Truth. We all get things right, and we all get things wrong. It is the human condition. Having said that, I will state my opinion on how we might be able to fix what is truly broken in America. Having said that, I believe the following to be faithful to the Truth.

I believe in the American Constitutional Republic and Truth with a capital T and Right vs. Wrong. We must have the courage to say so and not give in to the lie that everyone has their own Truth. They may have their reality, their perspective but not a separate truth; this cannot be stated strongly enough. Political correctness is nothing more than the fascism of language, an attempt to control your thoughts by limiting your words and changing how you think. While some words/phrases may be offensive, the first amendment right is that you get to use them no matter what anyone thinks.

The American founding fathers knew that people are sinful - not good. We know those good intentions cannot suffice for a legal standard of behavior. Well-intentioned is not the basis for law. Sadly human nature is the same as it has been since the beginning of humankind. The U.S. Constitution was developed with checks and balances on power for that very reason. To assume that people are good provides tyranny the ultimate breeding ground. Modern Humanism, which assumes humanity's goodness, is a religion complete with theology, liturgy, and its version of heaven and hell. Tenets of this religion are evolution, climate change, social engineering, globalism, and the elimination of religion. "Imagine" no religion, no governments… you get the idea. This idea of a liberal democracy that would emerge as some international dialectic has proven false.

I believe in God and that our founding fathers believed in a real God who ordained our new government, brought together (not by coincidence, as some would suggest) by the situations, political realities, histories – personal and general and the people who formed this nation. There was not some historical coincidence that led to our founding. Rather a deliberate and directed effort. I believe the founders knew building a great Christian Nation, not a theocracy, was why they were brought together in that time and place. The success of that endeavor would depend on maintaining our Judeo-Christian heritage; this is not to be confused with all Americans being Christians or how one defines being Christian. All people would/will benefit from this Godly Republic, whether Christian or not. That our Constitution provides Freedom of religion and from a forced one; that it also provides a codified Law for an honest and tangible Christian Liberty, whether Christian or not, that without the Judeo-Christian heritage that laid the foundation for and the same tradition that currently perpetuates the principals of our Republic; all would never have been or would now be lost.

That the ability of this Republic to be just and honest relies on the morality and ethics of the citizenry, whether Christian or not. One based on the rule of law. One cannot talk of fundamental Justice, authentic Liberty, Total Freedom, and real Prosperity without those who serve to be just and moral people. The Christian tradition provides the best example. We have lost this most essential tenet of our society. Let me make one crucial distinction here. When I speak of Christianity, I do not discuss America as a denominational theocracy. Please remember that Jesus was no lover of religion. He spent much of his time fighting the religion of his day, despite God having established Judaism and the old testament on which it is based. People have and will continue to try and decide what is and is not the accurate word of God through the plethora of denominations and religions out there. I am not wasting time on that here.

My beliefs dictate how I see what is wrong in America. How to "right the ship" is as well. The first step in repairing this Republic is to restore the family. Return Fathers to the family. Clearly, many facets are within the previous statement. The traditional family needs fixing. Yes, I know there is more than one type of family. My own was not traditional. It was common but not traditional. Too many children are missing the examples of mothers and fathers edifying a child's proper development.

Understand from the Judeo-Christin tradition that the family is the basis of government. The family is the first form of government ordained by God, established for the children's well-being and the essential building block of all society. In contemplating the Christian tradition's role in building this Constitutional Republic, it is crucial to understand the family's biblical and social function. Sadly, the State has ventured to take on the family's governance due to mothers and fathers' failure to "govern" the children or themselves. This becomes the basis for government replacing God from governing the family, being compassionate or benevolent. Handing this role to the government is no different from the Israelites building an idol rather than trusting in the God who had just delivered them. So, we have given up our Liberty because we no longer have the faith to exercise Liberty. On a theological note: Christians no longer enjoy full Christian Liberty's fullness because they lack the faith to exercise it. A whole loving family is what God and even nature have determined is best. Humankind has created other versions of the family to accommodate most people's failings, sins, and selfishness. Despite these failings, many people in many roles have stepped up to try and fill in those holes. I honestly believe that God will bless those people. After all, it is not the child's fault that their family may be broken. While there are justifications for these non-traditional families, the sad Truth is that, while it might be better than nothing, it is not the ideal.

Repairing the traditional family and pulling the government out of that role is an essential step. However, as a society, we must strive to prepare our children for the rigors of a functional and loving marriage. One in which a child can be nurtured and developed. Too many young men and young women have unreal expectations or underdeveloped skills for a valid partnership marriage. Having grown up in a single-parent(Mom) household, I was not as prepared as I should have been for my own marriage. Yet, I was determined to find that path. I was driven to be better as a husband and father. I write this acknowledging my own shortfalls. Not to condemn or find fault in others. Ironically, a proper family has a better chance of producing the preparation I speak of. The answers are pretty simple, but in no way are they easy. Under the most optimal of circumstances raising children and maintaining a loving, fulfilling family is not an easy task. Sadly, few people are operating within those optimal circumstances. Giving up on this ideal and abandoning it for what we have accepted now is admitting defeat.

Our education system has played a part in this systemic failure. Modern public education has attempted to fill the void and, in so doing, has made the family breakdown accelerate. Modern education must return to the role fr which it was established, to teach the elements of an educated child. Now, here is the excellent debate...what is an educated child? This could easily be a separate article, which it may. To attempt to keep it simple, from a school function. Let us assume that we speak of language, reading, writing, history (a complete telling), and of course, arithmetic, including the elements that branch out from these.

Our national education experiment is failing. This is not due to our front-line educators doing their best or, in many cases doing what they are told. While the inconsistencies between levels of education between states, urban and rural regions, attempting national standards, the curriculum has failed. Effective education needs to be local or regional at the minimum. The "education" that is going on today should happen in the family and local communities. Churches have also failed in the social education of children.

Solid families, better education, and more vital community involvement will likely produce better adults. These are the people we need to elect to public office of both parties. We have too many "leaders" suffering from delusions of grandeur or attempting to govern by feelings rather than logic and Truth. We are so thirsty for real, honest leadership that we have now mistaken popularity for leadership. We see this in our politics and all aspects of our lives. Why does an actor have any right to be an influencer in politics? Sports figures the same way. I never take my political cues from these people. Not that they are inherently bad, evil, or even wrong.

This leads me to another needed remedy. Where have all the statesmen/women gone? Our culture is currently void of statesmen and women. Our broken families, education systems, and communities have left us bereft of people capable of becoming our future statesmen. People who are adequately educated are called upon by God to lead. We are becoming a true democracy governed by those who are led by their feelings. Pure fad and whimsey are leading this country today. Hard decisions are best not made in this environment. I have touched on a mere fraction of what is broken and needs to be fixed. I will focus on these individually and a few more in future articles. All is not lost, there is hope, and with enough prayer and determination, we can put this country back on a surer footing.

Christian Times Magazine
EDORSES

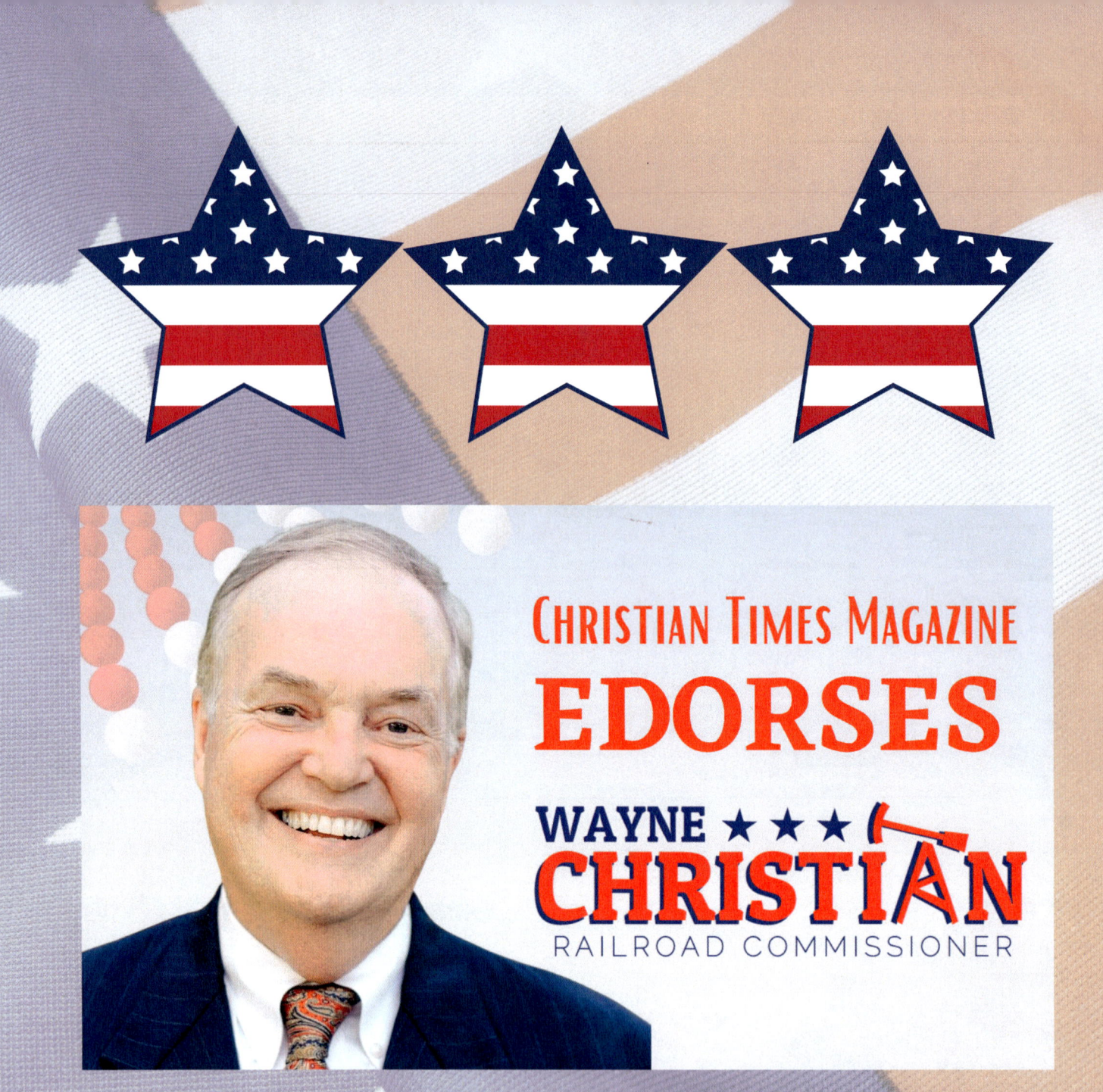

WAYNE ★★★ CHRISTIAN
RAILROAD COMMISSIONER

A CHANGE OF HEART BY GOD THE GREAT CARDIOLOGIST

By Dr. Georgette Nichols

I (and my Uncle Bill) listened to a sermon by Dr. John MacArthur about how if we believe in God we must also believe God controlled our emotions, our lives, our interactions and our hearts. Dr. MacArthur talked about how God was/is a Cardiologist. This spurred my desire and I decided to do some digging in all matters of the heart. I wished to learn about the heart shape origin, the origin of the word "heart" and the instances of heart in the Bible. The name and the heart shape/symbol resided in great curiosities and some conspiracies. These even went back to ancient lore.

Apollo was cited as the one who gave Greeks," the gift no one would forget", Silphium

artist depiction of what was believed to be the Silphium plant long since extinct

Hippocrates, the father of medicine, prescribed Silphium for a tummy tuck effect. Silphium was a plant similar to celery and from a similar genus Ferula. Why am I talking about an extinct celery-like plant in an article about the heart? The heart symbol is believed to be derived from the shape of the Silphium seed.

Silphium was many things; an aphrodisiac, an essential item of trade due to the resin, a spice for food and subsequently acted as an abortion pill. Rumor was the last existing Silphium plant was given to Nero. Even Julius Cesar was said to have stored the precious Silphium plants in his treasury… Later the image of the Silphium seeds would be embossed on coins and vases in lands conquered by the Romans.

Some references state the Greeks cultivated the plant mostly in Cyrene but the Romans learned to use the herb to the fullest potential perhaps as an abortion pill. A monthly dose of the Silphium seed, the size of a chickpea, was all that was needed to terminate a pregnancy.

Picture of Silphium seed embedded into an ancient coin. Put heart emoji next to it in article.

Silphium seed

Ironically today the Silphium seed on the coin has morphed into the heart emoji.

The lore of Silphium ends with the extinction of the seed due to increased consumption. The ancient civilizations actually ate the plant unto extinction! Now that the heart symbol (ironically from a medicinal plant) has been established let us examine the word heart. The Hebrew word for heart was often combined with a few other synonyms strung together for emphasis.

PSSF
© K. R. Robertson
Illinois Natural History Survey

Such can be seen in the Shema, a Jewish prayer. The Hebrew word for heart is levav or lev. Jewish people commonly pray the Shema which mentioned the word heart. The Biblical reference for the Shema is Deuteronomy 6:5-9; "Love the Lord your God will all your heart (levav or lev) and with all your soul and with all your strength (or might)." The Hebrew text does not mention the brain or mind as we understand them. The Hebrew text referenced the heart as the entire being of man- encompassing the mind. An interesting thing to note some state there is no exact Hebrew word for brain in the Bible. The closest word being lebab which translates to inner man, mind, will, or heart.

The word heart is mentioned in some translations of the Bible 826 times whereas the word brain is not mentioned once. God seems to be more concerned with the heart than the brain by mere reference. But as mentioned before in Hebrew language the mind (or brain?) and the heart are almost synonymous. Looking to Aristotle he said, "Educating the mind without educating the heart is no education at all." Something more intriguing can be seen with the heart when we study the origin and meaning in the English language. The etymology of the word heart stems from Old English heorte "heart (hollow muscular organ that circulates blood); breast, soul, spirit, will, desire; courage; mind, and intellect." The word heart regardless of the origin is defined the same. The more secular Shakespeare mentioned the heart many times and it was referenced in Macbeth; "False face must hide what the false heart doth know." This might be translated to modern day; a fakeness which resided in the heart has to be disguised by an outward face. The heart also gave life through God.

The heart as mentioned in the Bible gives you life. God can give you the desires of your heart. The Bible states the heart gives you life in Proverbs 4:23; "Keep your heart with all diligence, for out of it spring the issues of life." God wants us to keep our hearts with diligence focused on HIM and the Godly mission of life. Sometimes a change of heart is not directed toward God.

God being God controls all outcomes whether good or bad for HIS will while factoring in the heart's desire. This must be a huge endeavor. God can even change our heart's desires to fulfill HIS will. Deuteronomy 30:6 says; "And the Lord your God will circumcise your heart and the heart of your descendants, to love the Lord your God with all your heart." Circumcising the heart inferred God preformed an actual procedure on your heart/spirit which could affect the outcome of generations. God changed hearts in history as well; for example Ashoka of India. He waged a bloody war and burned 500 concubines to death then later regretted his evil. The regret was brought on when he gained a moral conscience in Buddhism. Sometimes the outcome of a changed heart was another religion sometimes it was towards God.

Sometimes a change of heart is away from good outcomes such as with Benedict Arnold. Benedict Arnold, a patriotic Major General, in the Revolutionary War betrays America later fighting for the British. Quite the change of heart Benedict. Do not forget the outcome of your choice was initiated and controlled by God in your heart. Fear not God looks at the heart not our appearance; 1 Samuel 16:7. In relation to God the heart and its complexity is quite bizarre and confusing for us mere mortals.

How do we know God still plans our steps revealing His will and our hearts desires regardless of our choices? Proverbs 16:9 states: "A man's heart plans his way. But the Lord directs his steps." A perfect example was Pharaoh. Exodus 7:3-4 "But I (God/Lord) will harden Pharaoh's heart and though I multiply my miraculous signs and wonders in Egypt, he will not listen to you…"

This was seen with Pharaoh and even President Biden who changed his heart toward abortion. Senator Biden once in 1982 voted to overturn Roe v. Wade but now seems assuaged otherwise- to kill the unborn. Both outcomes showed a hardened heart towards the goodness seen in God's will. A metamorphosis of the heart may be towards God! Regardless the outcome of the heart; God was/is in control. God even compared it to gambling but He has the house; Proverbs 16:33," The lot is cast into the lap, But its every decision is from the Lord."

God's will and your heart's desires also depends on your heart's programming. What we program to our heart coupled with God spurs the metamorphosis. Psalm 37:4 "Take delight in the Lord and He will give you the desires of your heart."
Knowing someone as omnipotent as God is in control of life's variables such as the heart's desire should bring us great comfort. This comfort should allow us to draw closer to Him. But we must search for God with our heart to achieve this comfort, peace and wholeness in God. If we search God will present himself, says Jeremiah 29:13, "And you will seek Me and find Me, when you search for ME with all your heart." The searching of the heart might cause a change of the heart; look at Saul/Paul in the New Testament he persecuted Christians to death then later became a Christian himself. The change occurred because of a visit from Jesus. Paul had a major change of heart. Paul died a martyr likely due to beheading

under the persecution of the Romans. This persecution was likely led by Nero. Who just so happened to love Silphium. If you do not know, the aphrodisiac loving Nero later killed himself to avoid his pending fate.

Another example of the heart's desire changed by the Lord can be seen with C.S. Lewis and my late Uncle Bill. Uncle Bill joined our God in Heaven June 7, 2022 before we finished this article together. He taught physics and math for over 50 years. He even tutored me throughout college so that I might complete my doctorate degree in pharmacy. One of the last things Uncle Bill and I spoke about was how to write about Dr. Macarthur's phrase uttered- God the Cardiologist. Uncle Bill and I had planned the outline together for this article while we both went our separate ways to research. I must confess most of my ideas for my articles stemmed from Saturday breakfast conversations with Uncle Bill or late night phone calls discussing the Bible and current events. I should mention our heart's desires change with us as we age. For example Uncle Bill began life following God and drifted away during college years like we all tend to do- C.S. Lewis and myself included. In college we tend to research the why and the how for the reasons of the World but ignore the WHO-GOD. Uncle Bill always calmly added in passing, "College and Doctorate programs are for affirming man as a God. Whereas the Bible shows you who God is and where He resides- your heart. "Uncle Bill would devote the last 25 years of his life to being a student in God's word. Uncle Bill would teach God's word during Sunday school and silently ghost write with me for Christian Times Magazine until his death. Consider this, both men in their youth may not have searched with their heart's to follow God's will for their life. Regardless the initial pursuit a change of heart occurred, C.S. Lewis would turn from atheist to God's child whereby writing Christian children's books. Subsequently because of his literature works; children would search for God with the desires of their hearts! Same might be said for Uncle Bill, to a smaller scale of course. He died writing alongside me about God. We wrote weaving current and past events with Scripture. Together we hoped for a pleasant narrative of mere words which might influence others to seek God with their hearts. Perhaps this article touched your heart. Remember to prepare our hearts for God. God told us distinctly in the Bible what we must do to keep our heart's focused on HIM; Proverbs 3:4 " Let not mercy and truth forsake you; Bind them around your neck, Write them on the tablet of your heart, Trust in the Lord with all you heart, And lean not on your own understanding. "

God reaffirmed through David in Psalms 31:24, "Be of good courage, and He shall strengthen your heart, all ye that hope in the Lord." We can gather strength from God if we seek Him. God orchestrates the programming and desires of our heart but also heals it through medicine. In fact in Proverbs 17:22; "A merry heart does good, like medicine, But a broken spirit dries the bones." God the Great Cardiologist not only preforms procedures but tells us what medicine will fix our heart.

CHRISTIAN TIMES MAGAZINE ENDORSES DR. JAMES RODGERS

VOTE

DOCTOR RODGERS
TEXAS CONSERVATIVE FOR CONGRESS
DISTRICT 30

PO BOX 84, LANCASTER, TX 75146
Team@jamesrodgersforcongress.com

Paid for by James Rodgers for Congress

By Zernalyn Palmares

MENTORS, LEADERS, TEACHERS AND GUIDES
THE VALUE OF MENTORING IN A CHRISTIAN PERSPECTIVE

During the 1400-1500's any form of a formal education was unusual . Children that were born of the peasant class during mid 1500's managed to attend some schooling of sort under the sponsorship of their Feudal lord with the understanding that they would go into the Lord's service , they would learn basic reading, math and ecclesiastical studies to eventually benefit the Fiefdom. But there was also the apprenticeship system, wherein a youth would work under the tutelage of a master craftsman for free in exchange for a valuable education . This individual lived under the roof of his mentor, ate what he ate, watched and observed and immersed himself in learning techniques , knowledge and skills that would serve as a trade to earn a living. Often times the master would take on the role of parent, guide and teacher providing their needs and moral direction.

In today's world wherein there is an eroding moral compass mentors that can lead and guide our youths into a biblical perspective of how to live their lives are far and few between. In a society that embraces worldly values, Christian mentoring has become an endangered social commodity. Teachers for fear of their jobs silently look on as prayer is taken away from schools and when holiday practices are stripped of their spiritual significance and replaced by commercialism.

During the 80's when watching Karate Kid, the perfect mentor would be Mr. Miyagi telling Daniel-San, "lie become truth only if person wanna believe it". Hollywood created a character that exemplified a strong moral compass. There was also a mutant rat named Splinter that would be the adoptive father of Teenage Mutant Ninja Turtles who would tell them " …happiness outside of yourself , you'll never find it . Happiness exists within you .."

But then again as good as this sounds is this in a biblical perspective ?

What is Christian Mentorship? According to Diane Partin, Behavioral Health Director (of Hospital System) . " For a Christian to mentor anyone, believers and non-believers, fulfils the gifts that God has given the Mentor. And the benefit to those mentored are being led by a person full of wisdom and love, who is seeking the best outcome for everyone through their leadership. Regardless, if scripture or God is discussed between Mentor and mentored. BUT if through this relationship a door is opened to discuss those things, then do so with gentleness, respect and love.... "speak the Truth in love." Ms. Partin quotes . For a Christian to mentor anyone, believers and non-believers, fulfils the gifts that God has given the Mentor. And the benefit to those mentored are being led by a person full of wisdom and love, who is seeking the best outcome for everyone through their leadership. Regardless if scripture or God is discussed between Mentor and mentored. BUT if through this relationship a door is opened to discuss those things, then do so with gentleness, respect and love.... "speak the Truth in love."

Ms. Partin quotes Ephesians 4: 1-16
As a prisoner for the Lord, then, I urge you to live a life worthy of the calling you have received. 2 Be completely humble and gentle; be patient, bearing with one another in love. 3 Make every effort to keep the unity of the Spirit through the bond of peace. 4 There is one body and one Spirit, just as you were called to one hope when you were called; 5 one Lord, one faith, one baptism; 6 one God and Father of all, who is over all and through all and in all.

7 But to each one of us grace has been given as Christ apportioned it. 8 This is why it[a] says:
"When he ascended on high,
he took many captives
and gave gifts to his people."[b]
9 (What does "he ascended" mean except that he also descended to the lower, earthly regions[c]? 10 He who descended is the very one who ascended higher than all the heavens, in order to fill the whole universe.) 11 So Christ himself gave the apostles, the prophets, the evangelists, the pastors and teachers, 12 to equip his people for works of service, so that the body of Christ may be built up 13 until we all reach unity in the faith and in the knowledge of the Son of God and become mature, attaining to the whole measure of the fullness of Christ.
14 Then we will no longer be infants, tossed back and forth by the waves, and blown here and there by every wind of teaching and by the cunning and craftiness of people in their deceitful scheming. 15

Instead, speaking the truth in love, we will grow to become in every respect the mature body of him who is the head, that is, Christ. 16 From him the whole body, joined and held together by every supporting ligament, grows and builds itself up in love, as each part does its work.

From good Christian Mentoring , Christian organizations thrive when their leaders have had the opportunity to be graced with the teachings of Christ . Covenant Kids Chief Operating Officer , Daniel Lund shares that " I am blessed to have some amazing mentors in my life currently that are not only strong advocates for the work we do but also support me on a personal level through love and accountability. I have learned so much and it is such an amazing feeling to have people who you can call on at any time for support. I hope to be able to give back to others what they have provided for me over the last several years.   The organization has nurtured more than 4,600 children in the past 15 years in foster family placements.

To build strong foundational faith future generations must learn from those that have come before them. Those that can impart the gift of lessons need to teach the children of tomorrow.
And even when I am old and gray, O God, do not forsake me, Until I declare your strength to this generation. Your power to all who are to come. Psalm 71:18

SAVE AMERICA
PRESIDENT DONALD J. TRUMP

- December 30, 2021 -

Endorsement of Sid Miller

Commissioner Sid Miller is a terrific Agriculture Commissioner for the Great State of Texas! A farmer and champion rodeo rider, Sid was an early fighter for our America First agenda. He is working hard to support our Farmers, Military and Vets, Lower Taxes, and Defend the Second Amendment. Sid has my Complete and Total Endorsement!

SID MILLER ENDORSED BY DONALD J. TRUMP

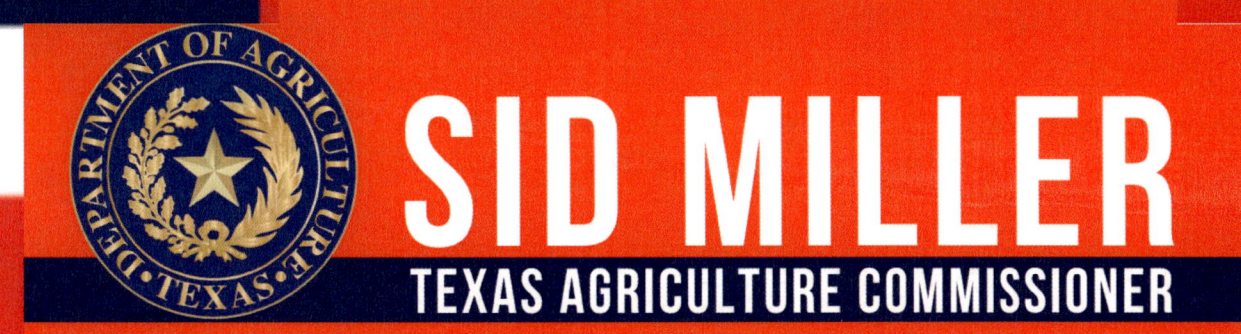

SID MILLER
TEXAS AGRICULTURE COMMISSIONER

YOUR VOTE. YOUR VOICE.

WEBSITE: WWW.MILLERFORTEXAS.COM
FACEBOOK PAGE: WWW.FACEBOOK.COM/MILLERFORTEXAS
TWITTER: @MILLERFORTEXAS

Paid for by Sid Miller Campaign

THIS AND THAT

By Mickey Nichols

It has been incredibly uplifting to watch the World Championships in Track and Field held for the last two weeks in Eugene, Oregon. The effort put forth by every single athlete at this event was glorious and the privilege of representing their country or nation exhibited by not only the winners but of every finisher was very noticeable. This is in vivid contrast to the so-called "stars" of professional sports who have gotten EXTREMELY wealthy by playing their sport in this country and then biting the hand that feeds them by continually rolling out the "race card" or the "gay bashing" card or the "non-inclusive card" (which can be anything they feel led to boo-hoo about !). I do know that the track athletes performing at the Worlds are, for the most part, also professionals, but not once did I see any one of these participants show anything but pride at the very mention of their country or nation. The joy of congratulating teammates was real and emotional and hugs and tears of gratitude were the order of the day. I found myself cheering just like I used to do from my living room couch as I watched event after event proceed in this fashion. It was heartwarming to witness this display of sportsmanship and thankfulness and rekindled a small ray of hope that there is still a chance for this sinful, perverted world to right its course and once again begin to do as God has directed us to do.

The recent passage of the Presidential Executive Order #14067 could very well sound the death knell for the United States of America. And after that, the entire world. You may well ask, what type of Order could possibly contain enough damage in its language to accomplish such a final blow for this country? Well, first I would direct you to read the Order for yourself by googling Executive Order #14067. You will find that its many items can be boiled down to a few hair-raising ideas that the "elites" such as Soros, Gates, and Zuckerburg, et al, have bonded together and directed the present Administration to implement as soon as possible. The two items that immediately caught my eye are these: 1) that President Biden has directed the DOJ, Treasury, and Dept. of Homeland Security (among others) to submit plans for the Federal Government to seize all cash assets in America and replace these cash assets with "digitized coin" assets and 2) that America implement a "social conscience score" rating system for every single citizen of the USA. This rating system, both handed out and managed by a special Governmental Department, would score everything and anything that anyone did. For example, because the "digitized coin" monetary system would contain miniaturized microchips that tracked each and every purchase that one made, citizens that bought goods and services not favored by "elites" would receive a low "social" score. Voting for the wrong candidate or party would lower one's "score". Putting gasoline into cars rather than having an electric car would lower the "score". Comments on FB, or Instagram, or Twitter that do not adhere to the "narrative" results in a low "score". And if you're not aware, this is the system that the Chinese populace lives with day in and day out. Jobs, promotions, enrollment at certain schools, are also determined by one's "score". Even getting a date with a certain person may depend upon one's "score"!

Far fetched, you say? The Department Heads of the various Cabinet positions have been given six to twelve months to report back to the President with their results. So, do not be surprised if this happens in late 2023 or certainly in 2024. I am not an alarmist. I merely report the facts as they are presented. Ask yourself this question: Are the people that are currently in charge capable of wanting to control all our actions to this degree? The answer, unfortunately, is a resounding YES. The puppeteers pulling the strings are shrewd and powerful men and ultimate control of everybody and everything is their goal.

Do not be fooled. All of #14067 (and other Executive Orders, such as #14027) are designed to be presented to the American public as simply ideas that will be good for the people. Lies can be couched in such terms that on the outside look safe and benign but inside are filled with deceit and the harm that can be done is not noticed until it is too late. Satan is the Father of lies and as such he leads his minions down roads that lead to destruction, both individuals and nations. It is no secret that the USA is now at a point where we are celebrating those things that Sodom and Gomorrah were destroyed for and that wrong is considered right and that right is now called wrong. Could any of us ever have believed that, for example, six to eight year old children would be physically desecrated by sex change operations and that these acts would be encouraged and approved by their own parents? God forbid. The ancient city of Nineveh was destined for utter destruction until the prophet Jonah preached God's warning to them and the entire peoples of the city repented of their sins. Because of this repentance God held up on His plan of destruction for another one hundred years. Of course, because the city once again fell into their old sinful ways.God then utterly destroyed it. I personally believe that America was on the brink of being totally swept away and forgotten in the annals of time but that the recent overthrow of Roe v. Wade may be a triggering event that calls our nation back to repentance. If we don't comply with God's commandments and we continue with our wicked ways then there is no hope. Because America was founded as a Christian nation and because it honored God in its documents initially I think that our country has always been favored by God. And because we have been known as a Christian nation then our judgment will be more severe when and if this happens. We stand at the edge of a cliff. Continued sin plunges us into the abyss but IF we repent of our sins and ask forgiveness then God MAY forego our punishment. I say MAY because America has had ample time and opportunity to change its direction but instead we have deepened our sin and now even flaunt it openly. The Roman Empire fell from within because of its degradation and corruption. Are we too far gone? Can America be saved? Time will tell.

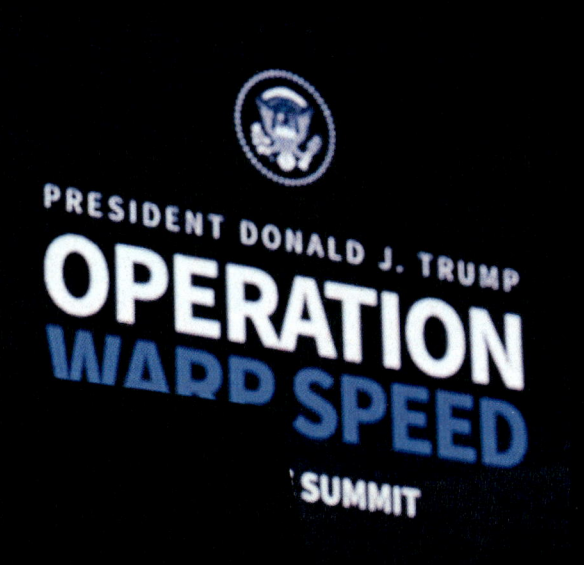

INTERVIEW WITH PAUL MANGO
TRUMP'S WHITE HOUSE FORMER DEPUTY CHIEF OF STAFF FOR POLICY

ANIL: Our guest today is Mr. Paul Mango who is a well-known personality, Thank you, Sir. for accepting our invitation.

Tell us about yourself!

PAUL: I was born in Albany, NY the Grandson of an Italian immigrant. Raised in an Italian/Irish catholic family, one of five siblings, son of a veteran,. When I was 18 years old, I went off to West Point and graduated as a member of the class of 1981. I was commissioned as a filed artillery officer and assigned to the 82nd Airborne Division at Fort Bragg, NC. My second assignment was in Germany with the 8th Infantry Division. After completing my service commitment, I attended the Harvard Business School. Upon graduation, I joined McKinsey & Company in

Pittsburgh, PA where I spent most of my career in the health care field. After a long career at McKinsey, I became a candidate for Governor in the Commonwealth of Pennsylvania. My run was not successful, but shortly thereafter I was asked to join the federal government in the Trump Administration as a senior official in the Department of Health and Human Services. I served there from 2018 until 2021 and spent my last full year there deeply involved with Operation Warp Speed. I subsequently wrote a book about my experience with Warp Speed and it is due out in June of 2022.

ANIL: Where were you born and raised?

PAUL: Born in Albany, NY and lived there until I was 4 years old. Thereafter, I lived in Syracuse, NY where I attended public primary and secondary schools. When I left for West Point at age 18, I never lived full-time again in Syracuse.

ANIL: Where were you educated?

PAUL: Earned a BS at the United States Military Academy at West Point and an MBA from Harvard Business School

ANIL: What is the status of your current political persuasions?

PAUL: Conservative. I have supported conservative candidates for the last couple of decades. While not active in politics as a candidate, I stay in touch with several Senators and Representatives

ANIL: Would you call yourself a conservative Republican? If so, how long have you been a part of the Republican party and how have you served in the party?

PAUL: Been a conservative Republican since President Reagan handed me my diploma when I graduated from West Point in 1981. President Reagan had a significant influence on me because he came into office during a time when the Country was not doing well and he quickly addressed a number of pressing issues and the Country recovered spectacularly well. I agreed with his free market principles and his commitment to a strong defense.

ANIL: Tell us about your work and the Trump campaign and your work and the Trump administration

PAUL: I served in the Department of Health and Human Services both as the Chief of Staff at CMS and Deputy Chief of Staff at HHS. During this time, we propagated a number of regulations designed to empower the healthcare consumer and give him more choice. In fact, the theme of our administration's approach to improving healthcare was "Choice and Competition". One of the most significant regulations we propagated health with increasing price transparency such that every American would know what a medical procedure cost before the procedure was performed. We also dealt with the epidemic of Electronic Nicotine Delivery Systems (ENDS), otherwise known as vape devices. Companies were aggressively marketing these devices to high school children and we saw the level of nicotine addiction skyrocket in 2017 and 2018. Thereafter, we precluded these companies from marketing the devices to children. Of course, in January of 2020, the global COVID-19 pandemic hit our shores and we spent the entire balance of our administration dealing with it.

ANIL: How long have you been associated with the former president, Donald Trump?

PAUL: Since 2018 when I became part of his administration. I had the privilege of meeting with him several times while I was in the administration

ANIL: Since the 2020 campaign what has been your involvement in the political realm?

PAUL: Composing a book about Operation Warp Speed and describing my time with President Trump during that operation. As I mentioned, I follow politics closely and support political candidates, but other than that I am not actively involved in politics presently.

ANIL: What would you say your current job is; and how are you working today and politics?

PAUL: I am a board member of several health care companies; some of which are private, but others publicly-traded. I also play a number of advisory roles to healthcare executives. Lastly, I am promoting my book on Operation Warp Speed. The Country needs to know how the Trump Administration, in conjunction with its private sector partners, saved millions of American lives by bringing safe and Effective time vaccines to market more quickly than anytime in

ANIL: Tell us about your family; are you married and have children?

PAUL: Married for 40 years to the same woman. My wife in a graduate of West Point as well in the class of 1982. Five daughters ages 34,31,29,26, and 18. All of my daughters are pursuing exciting careers or finishing their studies at college

ANIL: Do you have any political aspirations for the future? If so, tell us about them….

PAUL: If asked, I would serve again in the Federal Government in the next Republican Administration. I have no aspirations to run for elected office again.

ANIL: Have you ever ran for political office? If so, tell us about your campaigns…

PAUL: Candidate for Governor of the Commonwealth of PA, 2018. I was not very well-known in Pennsylvania politics at the time and I was not supported by the State party. But, I mounted an insurgent campaign and wound up 6 points short of the winner. I like to say that I did not lose, it's just that the clock ran out on me.

ANIL: Are you currently involved in any political campaigns in any way, shape, or form? If so, tell us of your involvement…

PAUL: Supporting multiple Republican Senate candidates financially, but I am not involved directly in any campaigns.

ANIL: Can you please tell us of your relationship with Donald Trump and his campaigns? And do you foresee him running for President in 2024?

PAUL: No idea about his 2024 plans. He did call me to congratulate me on my book about Operation Warp Speed

ANIL: For quite some time now, we have wanted to gain an interview with Mrs. Trump, the former presidents' wife. Is it possible that you can help us secure this interview?

PAUL: No idea about his 2024 plans. He did call me to congratulate me on my book about Operation Warp Speed

ANIL: Is there anything else you would like to tell our readers? We have more than 880,000 readers in North America; I am sure I would like to hear you speak further of the former president, and we all love and admire. And we want to

PAUL: Just that I am delighted to be able to do an interview with the Christian Times and consider it a privilege to have served the American People as part of the Trump Administration

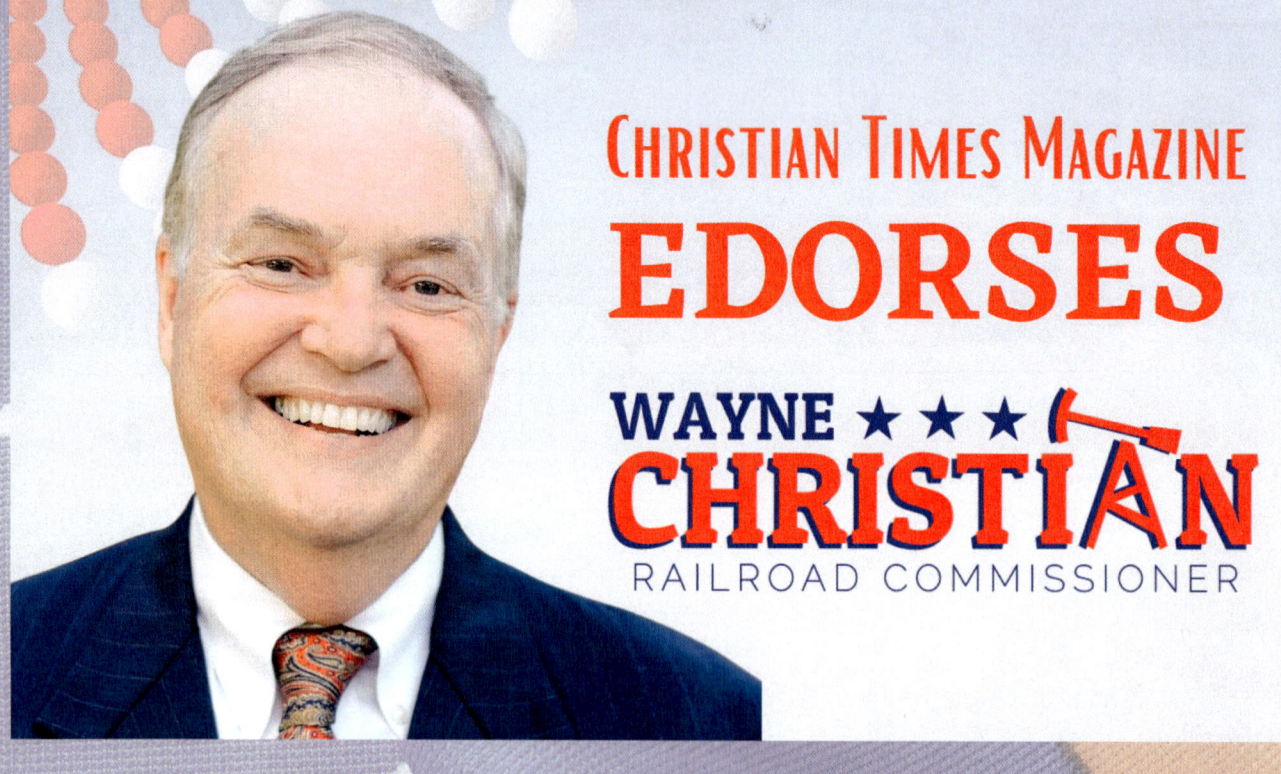

Christian Times Magazine
EDORSES

WAYNE ★★★ CHRISTIAN
RAILROAD COMMISSIONER

SAVE AMERICA
PRESIDENT DONALD J. TRUMP

December 30, 2021

Endorsement of Sid Miller

Commissioner Sid Miller is a terrific Agriculture Commissioner for the Great State of Texas! A farmer and champion rodeo rider, Sid was an early fighter for our America First agenda. He is working hard to support our Farmers, Military and Vets, Lower Taxes, and Defend the Second Amendment. Sid has my Complete and Total Endorsement!

SID MILLER ENDORSED BY DONALD J. TRUMP

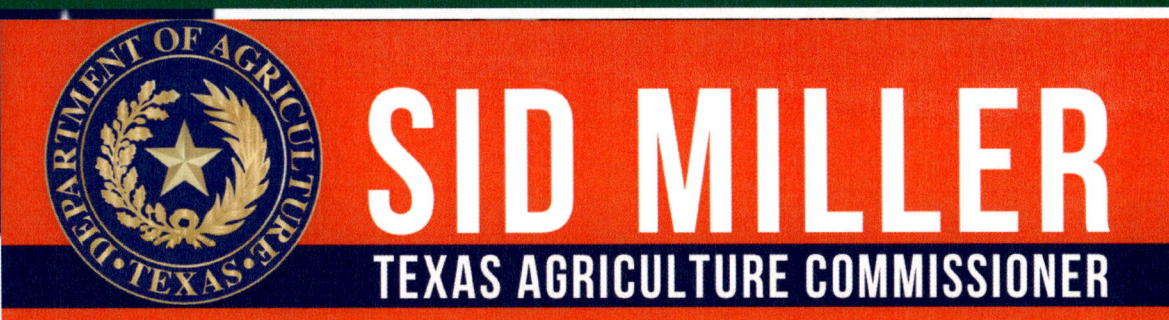

SID MILLER
TEXAS AGRICULTURE COMMISSIONER

YOUR VOTE. YOUR VOICE.

WEBSITE: WWW.MILLERFORTEXAS.COM
FACEBOOK PAGE: WWW.FACEBOOK.COM/MILLERFORTEXAS
TWITTER: @MILLERFORTEXAS

Paid for by Sid Miller Campaign

Made in United States
Orlando, FL
26 August 2022